Making the Most of

WORK EXPERIENCE

Making the Most of
WORK EXPERIENCE

Lois Graessle
Patricia McQuade

CAMBRIDGE UNIVERSITY PRESS
Cambridge   New York   Port Chester   Melbourne   Sydney

Published by the Press Syndicate of the University of Cambridge
The Pitt Building, Trumpington Street, Cambridge CB2 1RP
40 West 20th Street, New York, NY 10011, USA
10 Stamford Road, Oakleigh, Melbourne 3166, Australia

First published 1990

Printed in Great Britain at the University Press, Cambridge

British Library cataloguing in publication data
McQuade, Patricia
   Making the most of work experience.
   1. Great Britain. Secondary schools. Students.
   Work experience. Attitudes of teachers
   I. Title   II. Graessle, Lois
   373.2′7′0941

ISBN 0 521 357292

Acknowledgements

The authors would like to thank:
   Jenny Edwards, ILEA Divisional Industry School Co-ordinator
   Sue Karahalli and staff of Southwark College
   Chris Ireland, North Westminster Community School
   Mike Bees, Training Education Development Consultants
   Kerry Davy John, Southwark College
   Susan Luckins for the cartoon illustrations
   Cover design and illustration by Joanne Barker

Contents

"Work Experience – in which pupils carry out particular jobs more or less as would a regular employee though with emphasis on the educational aspect of the experience."

"Work Experience as such is governed by the Education (Work Experience) Act 1973."

"Every pupil should have the opportunity before leaving school to have experienced directly the realities of working life."

(from Education at Work – A Guide for Schools, *Department of Education and Science, 1988)*

Introduction

Making the Most of Work Experience is a practical guide to help teachers plan and deliver a work experience programme.
Work experience affords exciting, enjoyable, learning opportunities to pupils and students provided both they and the employers are prepared, the scheme is well-organized, and the whole is fully integrated into the curriculum.

Teachers often remark on the new skills and added confidence developed during work experience.

Although it has its rewards, for teachers the organization of work experience can be demanding. It highlights the many-faceted, multi-skilled role of schoolteachers and college lecturers who are called upon to be managers, curriculum developers, tutors, administrators, negotiators and trouble shooters.

This book begins by looking at this complex role in the context of work experience. It examines the tasks teachers are called upon to carry out and identifies the skills and knowledge needed. It gives a framework for in-service training and an analysis of training needs for formulating personal staff development plans. It then takes teachers step by step through the design, preparation and delivery of a work experience programme.

Teachers should work through the chapters on their own or with their course team. Because every teacher's situation is diffcrent, activities are provided at various stages of the text to allow the individual teacher to focus on how best, in his/her school or college, to use the many suggestions, guidelines and student assignments, and make the most of work experience.

Most of this book is about employer-based work experience. Recognising that circumstances may prevent some teachers from mounting such a scheme, the final chapter looks at alternatives such as mini-companies and work simulations.

1. Work Experience

A Complex Undertaking

Work experience makes many demands on teachers' skills and energies. Organizing and delivering a work experience programme requires flexibility, ingenuity and enterprise. It calls for the ability to handle a multi-faceted role, and skill in reconciling the different, sometimes conflicting, aspects.

When organizing and delivering a work experience scheme teachers wear three different hats:

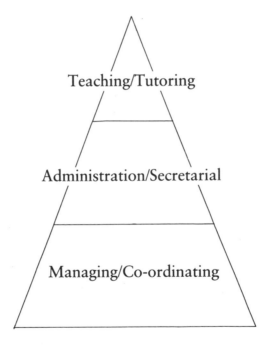

Teaching/Tutoring

Administration/Secretarial

Managing/Co-ordinating

This chapter sets out to summarize the roles, skills and tasks involved in these three main aspects of work experience provision. It aims to give an overall picture of the demands of work experience so that teachers can judge how past experience can be relevant and useful. It helps to show where further training and staff development are needed to develop new expertise.

Sometimes the tasks may be divided up amongst a course team or shared with other staff. At other times a single teacher will be responsible for work experience. Whichever is the case, work experience is a complex undertaking.

1. Teaching/Tutoring

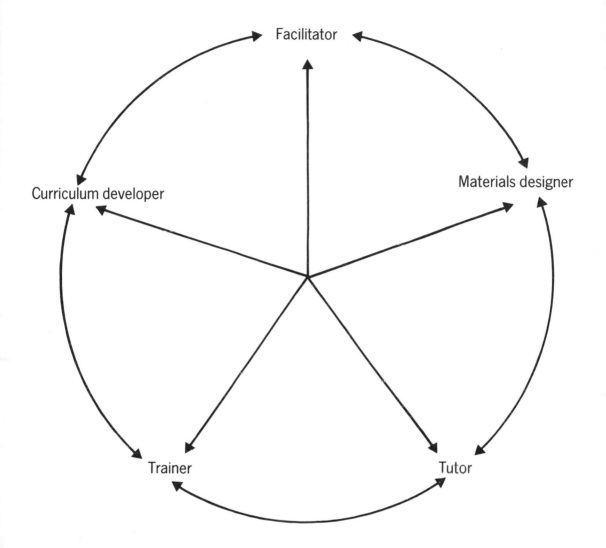

Work experience has the greatest educational and vocational significance when designed and delivered as an integral part of the curriculum. The teacher's skills as a curriculum developer are brought fully into play by the challenge this represents. Work experience placements need, as far as is practicable, to be the result of discussion, dialogue and negotiation with students. Ideally, each student's placement should be custom-built to meet his or her educational and vocational aspirations. It should represent the result of careful analysis and preparation in the timetable before the work experience programme begins.

T

Once the programme is in operation the teacher will be the major source of support for students, work sponsors and any staff from external agencies involved in the programme network. The teacher's professional skills in teaching and tutoring young people will now have to be transferred and applied in ways and in settings very different from those of the classroom.

2. Administrative/Secretarial

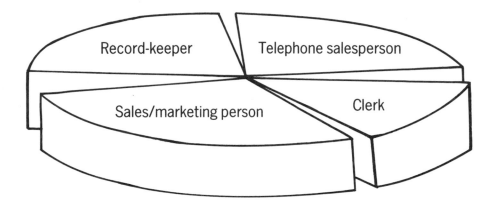

It is possible to fall into the trap of thinking that once work placement providers have been established and students have been positioned in the workplace, all that remains is for the teacher to make the occasional visit to see that everything is running smoothly.

Instead, teachers can expect a significant increase in correspondence, telephone calls, messages, crisis signals from the field, flows of cash vouchers and cheques to pay for travel, lunches and materials, and sometimes demands for special clothing and equipment. All this has to be accounted for in more than just an informal way. In fact, a work experience scheme will be heavily dependent for its success on a solid foundation of efficient administrative and secretarial back-up.

Everyone involved in a work experience programme needs to be briefed as fully on the use of the administrative system as they are on the visits to work experience. A message gone astray can mean the difference between a problem at the workplace being dealt with in time and a crisis that could leave a student without a placement.

3. Managing/Co-ordinating

Planner

People and resources manager

Trouble shooter

Mediator

Evaluator

Team leader

'Buck holder'

Although teachers are sometimes reluctant to don the label of 'manager', nevertheless, a work experience scheme is a complex enterprise whose various components require managing/co-ordinating/overseeing/ supervising – call it what you will.

Management will not be as new or different a role as it sounds. Teachers often underestimate the management skills they develop in the course of their everyday work, both in the classroom and in the wider institution.

These skills are nowhere more in evidence than in the provision of work experience.

Activities for the Teacher

Most teachers in the early days of work experience learned to juggle these various aspects by being thrown in at the deep end. By now it should be possible to anticipate some of what will be required. The following activities look at the tasks and skills required to plan and carry out work experience. They should help teachers in assessing their skills to date and in identifying means of support, delegation and in-service training.

1. Take the three aspects of organising and delivering work experience listed below, and jot down the tasks you think might feature under each heading for work experience in your setting:

(a) Teaching/tutoring;
(b) Administrative/secretarial;
(c) Managing/co-ordinating.

2. The basis of this activity is a task breakdown of work experience drawn from the experience of many teachers who have run work experience programmes. Compare your ideas with theirs, recognizing that each list is likely to be slightly different because of different institutions, education authorities, course requirements, and local custom and practice.

Using the task breakdown below, see how your own experience will help in implementing a work experience programme. In each of the spaces note for each task listed:

(a) a similar task you have undertaken in the course of your teaching or other work;

(b) a significant difference between the task you have noted and the work experience task.

For example:

Task	Similar task you have undertaken	Significant difference for work experience
presenting work experience to students and, where appropriate, to parents	introducing residential	students are in company, not with teachers, no money needed

1. TEACHING/TUTORING

Task	Similar task you have undertaken	Significant difference for work experience
1. determine aims and objectives of work experience		
2. build work experience into students' programmes		
3. integrate work experience with school/college-based elements of students' programmes		
4. present work experience to students and, where appropriate, parents		
5. prepare students for work experience placements by developing active learners who can recognize opportunities and appropriate methods of learning		
6. produce or purchase learning materials		
7. provide opportunities for students to acquire relevant vocational skills and knowledge		

Task	Similar task you have undertaken	Significant difference for work experience
8. build students' self-confidence		
9. introduce students to ways in which they can assess and record their own learning and progress during placements		
10. negotiate placement choice with students		
11. raise awareness and develop strategies for dealing with such practical consequences on work experience of, e.g., sexism, racism		
12. review student progress on placement and work through any problems		
13. record achievement: work with students on their portfolios, progression plans		
14. ensure that work experience is related to future education and job plans		

2. ADMINISTRATIVE/SECRETARIAL

Task	Similar task you have undertaken	Significant difference for work experience
1. design and dispatch all necessary correspondence and documentation		
2. find work experience placements		
3. liaise with other schools, colleges, interested agencies regarding work experience arrangements		
4. make placement arrangements clear to students, sponsors, parents, colleagues		
5. arrange students' initial visits to work sponsors		
6. plan a tutor placement visit schedule		
7. provide a telephone communication link between work sponsors and students on placement and yourself and others at school/college		
8. keep written records as required		
9. administer work experience-related finance and expenditure for staff and students		
10. prepare written reports for various committees, e.g. convening committee, working parties where necessary, minutes/statistics for governors		

3. MANAGING/CO-ORDINATING

Task	Similar task you have undertaken	Significant difference for work experience
1. determine and monitor standards and quality of programme		
2. obtain, allocate and be accountable for resources		
3. allocate tasks and responsibilities between yourself, team, other staff involved		
4. co-ordinate overall development and progress of scheme		
5. take responsibility for health and safety management within work experience programme		
6. manage public relations and liaison: involvement and consultation with trade unions, links with local industry and commerce and with other schools, colleges, MSC where appropriate		
7. ensure a policy of equal opportunities pervades all aspects of work experience scheme and devise strategies for dealing with problems in practice		
8. evaluate scheme		
9. ensure the scheme is recorded, systematic and institutionally recognized so that it is not dependent upon any particular teacher(s) and so that continuity can be guaranteed despite staff changes		

3. Look at the list of broad skills needed to carry out each of the three aspects of work experience provision. Put a tick in the appropriate box to indicate:

(a) a skill which you have already developed and which you are confident can be easily transferred into the context of work experience provision;
(b) a skill in which you have some practice but where you will need more support to use it in a work experience context;
(c) a skill which you have not yet developed, or one which you have tried to develop and found very difficult, where you will definitely need some further training and staff development.

Refer back to your notes in **Activity 2** to make sure you are doing yourself justice. You may find that a simple tick is not precise enough for you. If not, score yourself on a scale of 1 (low) to 5 (high) within each box instead.

1. TEACHING/TUTORING

Skills	Confident can use in work experience	Some practice; can use with support	Do not have skill; need training
1. determine and write aims and objectives			
2. monitor and review assessments made by work sponsors to the performance criteria set by relevant body, e.g. RSA, City and Guilds			
3. design, produce and/or select learning materials			
4. use communication skills to sell an idea			
5. facilitate: meetings, groupwork			
6. counsel/tutor: formal/ informal			
7. use role-play and simulation			

2. ADMINISTRATIVE/SECRETARIAL

Skills	Confident can use in work experience	Some practice; can use with support	Do not have skill; need training
1. plan overall scheme, visits, etc.			
2. prioritize			
3. liaise with colleagues, work sponsors, MSC, etc.			
4. organize visits, in-service training			
5. market and sell			
6. use telephone sales techniques			
7. teach self-presentation techniques			
8. design/formulate letters and forms			
9. type/word-process			
10. file/keep records			

3. MANAGING/CO-ORDINATING

Skills	Confident can use in work experience	Some practice; can use with support	Do not have skill; need training
1. formulate policy and operational plans			
2. communicate plans to others and get their co-operation			
3. make decisions			
4. manage time, people, conflict, stress			
5. delegate jobs, responsibilities			
6. prioritize			
7. give leadership in appropriate style			
8. see things through to completion			
9. use evaluation and review skills			

4A. If you are organizing a work experience scheme on your own:

(i) Review the outcomes of **Activities 1, 2,** and **3.**
(ii) Prioritize the areas of work and skills that you most need to develop in order to manage your work experience scheme.
(iii) Make an action plan for the in-service training/staff development you need and the support you might draw on for advice, help, etc. Be realistic: it is wise to set yourself no more than seven priorities for the year, so try to identify which areas and skills *for you* are most important to give you the confidence to do the job. Use the following headings:

Priorities	In-service Training/ Staff Development (when, arrangements)	Support (who, when)

4B. If you are organizing a work experience scheme as a team or group:

(i) Review the first three activities individually, prioritizing the seven areas of work or skills which you feel are most important for your own development in the role you are carrying out.

(ii) Share the results of the review with the others involved in planning and implementing your scheme.

(iii) Set group priorities for joint training and identify routes and methods of staff development/in-service training for individuals, as well as support available both within and outside the group.

2. An Educational Framework

Aims, Objectives and Qualifications

This chapter sets the educational framework for work experience. It discusses questions teachers must answer before embarking upon the practical details of planning and delivering placements for their students:

- How does work experience fit into the overall curriculum?
- What are the learning opportunities offered by work experience?
- What is the aim of this particular work experience scheme?
- What will be the students' learning objectives?
- How will these objectives be translated into placement programmes for each student?
- How will students' learning and achievement be assessed, reviewed and recorded?

Recognizing the Learning Opportunities

Work experience provides opportunities for experiential learning through which students can:

1. experience the culture of working life;
2. prepare for the transition to work;
3. discover their own occupational preferences;
4. learn and practise occupational skills;
5. demonstrate occupational competence;
6. work and learn in a novel environment;
7. enhance their motivation to learn;
8. build self-confidence;
9. develop personal effectiveness and enterprise skills;
10. practise basic/core skills in the context of work.

The degree of emphasis teachers wish to place on each on these opportunities will differ according to the part work experience plays within their overall curriculum planning. Teachers working with fifth year GCSE pupils destined to leave school in the summer might use work experience as primarily providing opportunities 1, 2, 3, 4, 8 and 9. A Special Needs tutor designing a work experience programme may look especially for placements offering opportunities 6, 7, 8, 9, 10. Youth

Training, whilst utilising opportunities 8, 9 and 10, will place particular emphasis on 4 and 5.

Lecturers in further education whose students are following courses leading to National Vocational Qualifications (NVQs) will look to work experience placements to afford students the opportunity to demonstrate that they can successfully apply their skills and knowledge to specified national standards in the workplace – in other words, opportunity number 5. TVEI tutors in schools may also hope that work experience will give their pupils a chance to work towards demonstrating the competence elements required to achieve units of credit towards National Vocational Qualifications.

The first step then for teachers in designing a work experience programme is to identify and prioritize the learning opportunities that they wish their work placements to deliver – to set out clearly the *aim* of the work experience scheme. The next step is to set out the learning objectives.

Setting Out the Learning Objectives

These will be the students' learning goals for the period of their work experience placements. Some may be applicable to all placements, e.g.

- to arrive on time;
- to work well with other people;
- to demonstrate initiative when appropriate;
- to ask questions when uncertain;
- to finish off tasks properly;
- to observe health and safety regulations.

Other learning goals will be specific, relating to placements in particular occupational areas, e.g. business and office placements, catering, engineering, retail placements.

Where the learning opportunities emphasized are numbers 4 and 5, then these occupational learning goals are particularly significant. However, whatever the learning opportunities prioritized by a scheme, it is still important that teachers, students and placement providers have a clear statement of exactly what tasks the student will perform during the time of the placement and to what standard.

In stating these goals, teachers may usefully consider adopting the language of *competence* used in National Vocational Qualifications, even if their students are not actively involved in seeking such qualifications.

The NVQ Format and the Language of Competence

National Vocational Qualifications are statements of occupational competence. The awards are given for demonstration of competence to standards set by Industry. The awards are expressed in the form of units of competence – groups of related tasks that a person should be able to perform in order to be deemed competent in a range of work roles in a particular occupational sector, for example, Clerical and Business Administration, Catering. These tasks are called elements of competence.

But it is not enough to be able to do a task. In National Vocational Qualifications, the way it must be done is clearly spelt out. It must be done to the *national standard* which has been set by the industry itself.

These standards are expressed as *performance criteria* which must be satisfied before a person can be assessed as competent at a task. Being competent means being able to carry out a task consistently to the stated performance criteria in the workplace. It is about knowledge, skill, and the application of that knowledge and skill in real work situations. Here are some examples of NVQ elements of competence and performance criteria:

ELEMENT OF COMPETENCE: Make telephone calls

Performance criteria: Correct telephone number obtained and contact established
Purpose of call clearly stated
Information accurately relayed as appropriate
Faults reported promptly
Approved working practices met

ELEMENT OF COMPETENCE: Receive and direct visitors

Performance criteria: Visitors greeted politely with a smile
Appropriate questions asked to establish purpose of the visit
Identification of person/product/service established
Appropriate person notified
Appropriate documentation completed if necessary
Visitors directed/ accompanied to correct location
Approved working practices met
(from National Retail Council NVQ Level 2)

In setting out students' learning goals for work experience, teachers can take the same starting points as National Vocational Qualifications:

- What tasks should the students be able to do by the end of the work experience?
- To what standard should they be able to do them?

Units of competence already drawn up by different industries may prove very useful and save teachers a lot of work as they can pick out competence elements and performance criteria relevant to their own students and their own placements. Useful addresses for obtaining such information appear at the end of this chapter.

Other advantages to using the NVQ format are:

- employers are becoming increasingly familiar with it and so it will be helpful when negotiating placements and planning placement programmes;
- it will allow students in the future to make maximum use of any assessments made of their achievement during work experience;
- if appropriate to do so, it will allow students to gain credits towards National Vocational Qualifications;
- it provides a simple, straightforward basis for assessing and recording student achievement on work experience.

How this framework will be used in scheme design will depend on the particular learning opportunities of work experience which teachers have chosen to maximize. For some schemes, the achievement of competence – the application of skills and knowledge in the workplace – will be paramount as students seek units of competence towards National Vocational Qualifications. For other schemes, the focus will be more on the learning processes than on the end achievement. Teachers will want to see students working towards rather than necessarily achieving any particular occupational competence. They will be looking for evidence of problem-solving, sustaining interest and enthusiasm, and of coping with working in the adult world. Students may have projects to complete which aim to enable them to learn about the world of work in general rather than master occupational skills in particular.

Nevertheless, students will be doing real work tasks during their time on placement and not to assess and record the occupational tasks they perform is to undersell work experience and undervalue student achievement. A work experience programme drawn up in terms of elements of competence and performance criteria will be of equal use to both types of scheme. The difference in emphasis will be in how the documentation is used and to what end.

Designing a Work Experience Programme

Statements of learning goals, both general and occupationally specific, can be put to good
use in:

    (a) negotiating placements with employers;
    (b) designing placement programmes.

Both of these are dealt with in more detail later in the book (see Chapter 4).

At this stage, what must be done is to design the documentation that will enable placement seekers to explain to employers what the required competence elements for students are in a particular occupational area and then to ask:

- In which of these elements of competence do you think you can provide opportunites?
- How, in what context, would the student learn/practise this particular element of competence?
- Can we draw up a programme of activity for the placement that will give the student:

(a) opportunities to learn these tasks;

(b) opportunities to practise these tasks;

(c) (if appropriate) opportunities to demonstrate competence in these tasks?

- Which parts of the tasks which we have agreed will form the basis of the placement can our students learn from you? Which do we need to teach them first so they can then practise with you?
- Are your staff used to training young people? Is there anything we can do to help?

Assessing and Recording Learning and Achievement on Work Experience

The assessment of achievement on work experience will be the task of the placement provider or supervisor in negotiation with the student. If teachers use the format suggested earlier in this chapter, then what the placement provider is asked to do is very clearly stated – to assess whether the student is competent at a task, e.g.

- Has the student consistently met the stated performance criteria?
- Is the student working well towards achieving competence in the task but is in need of further training or practice?

Teachers may wish to design additional documentation to help in the process of recording progress towards competence. Guidelines, too, can be drawn up regarding assessment techniques, stressing that assessment is to be continuous and not a one-off test especially set up for the student. The idea of demonstrating competence is to be able to do the task to the standard consistently.

Reviewing Student Progress

A placement review method is most easily designed in conjunction with a system for tutor visits to students during their placements. Student and tutor can discuss how the placement programme is going and, with the placement provider, monitor the student's progress and achievement. This review can also be the point at which the continuous assessments which placement providers have been making can be recorded. Many placement providers shy away from paper work, so teachers can help out here with detailed writing up of notes made by placement providers on student achievement.

In Conclusion

Sometimes, in the past, teachers saw work experience as peripheral to the mainstream curriculum, a heaven-sent relief from the daily routine of the classroom, a chance to get through some marking or even curriculum development whilst the students were away for two or three weeks. Most of the students had an enjoyable time away from school or college, some learned something of general utility and, for many, self-confidence grew.

Nowadays, there is a developing recognition of the significance of work experience as a route towards vocational competence. Experience gathered on placement is regarded as an important part of the accumulated evidence of achievement for certification. This can only happen when the learning objectives of the work experience programme are carefully worked out and clearly articulated, and if a co-ordinated, integrated system of assessing, reviewing and recording student progress and achievement is designed and implemented.

Activities for the Teacher

1. Identify and prioritize the learning opportunities of work experience in terms of your own particular scheme.

Discuss and draft as a statement of intent the aim of your work experience scheme.

2. Identify the occupational areas in which placements in your scheme will occur. Draw up a list of learning goals — elements of competence which students might attempt to gain during their placements. Use elements of competence identified by Training Boards and others for National Vocational Qualifications as a basis for this. Useful addresses are included at the end of the chapter.

Occupational Area	
Competence Elements	Performance Criteria

Note the performance criteria for each element of competence.

The lists you draw up will act as a basic document when negotiating placements, identifying what placements can offer, and drawing up a programme of how it will be offered.

3. If you do not already know about them, find out about National Vocational Qualifications. Read some of the literature suggested in the Bibliography.

4. Make sure you have a clear idea of what you want students to learn in their placements, how this will be assessed, and how the assessments will be recorded, before you go on to work through the rest of this book, planning the shape of your programme and carrying it out.

SOME USEFUL ADDRESSES

National Council for
Vocational
Qualifications
222 Easton Road
London NW1 2BZ

Engineering Industry
Training Board
PO Box 176
41 Clarendon Road
Watford
Herts WD1 1LB

Hotel and Catering
Training Board
International House
High Street
Ealing
London W5 5DB

National Retail
Training Council
c/o Retail Consortium
Commonwealth House
1–19 New Oxford
Street
London WC1A 1PA

Construction Industry
Training Board
Dewhurst House
24 West Smithfield
London EC1A 9JA

Royal Society of Arts
John Adam Street
London WC2N 6EZ

City and Guilds of
London Institute
76 Portland Place
London W1N 4AA

Business and Technician
Education Council
Central House
Upper Woburn Place
London WC1H 0HH

3. Equal Opportunities Issues for Work Experience

'... equal opportunities need not be a problem ...'

An equal opportunities policy must underpin work experience for both educational and legal reasons. Teachers preparing students for work experience need to encourage them to develop their potential, without conventional restrictions. Students need placements which are not limited by race, sex, disability, or culture.

Because of their dependence on placements offered by local employers, many work experience organisers face the dilemma of whether, in order to secure placements for other students, to collude with an employer who will not, for example, accept girls or black students.

Legislation and legal action show that not only are firms liable to prosecution if they contravene the Race Relations or Sex Discrimination Acts in work experience placements, but that schools and colleges themselves may be at risk of prosecution if they knowingly accept such a contravention.

This chapter will focus specifically on the role of an equal opportunities policy in work experience, on strategies to encourage students to face these issues, and on the legal implications.

Equal Opportunities in the School or College

A conference of teachers involved in work experience at a large inner city college recently concluded that, without the support of a stated equal opportunities policy and the commitment of senior management to it, what they could do individually to support equal opportunities amongst their students was extremely limited.

Many schools and colleges have or are formulating equal opportunities policies. It can be helpful to have the policy spelled out with particular reference to work experience. Here is one college's equal opportunities code of practice for work experience organizers and statements of equal opportunities for employers and students.

Equal Opportunities Code of Practice for Work Experience Organizers

As part of good educational practice, Southwark College is committed to offering equal opportunities to all its students in all aspects of their courses, including work experience.

During 1987 an employer was successfully prosecuted by the Commission for Racial Equality for refusing to take black school students on work experience. Although as yet there have been no similar prosecutions for refusing to offer women placements, this would be equally illegal. Under Section 42 of the Sex Discrimination Act a student who is refused a work experience placement because of his or her sex has the right to prosecute the company. If the College goes along with the employer's wishes, the student has the right also to prosecute the College.

Negotiating Placements with Students

In negotiating work experience with students, staff should:

> 1. Not make assumptions about students entering traditional sex-stereotyped jobs on work experience.
> 2. Offer students the possibility of entering non-traditional placements and promote its value in terms of making a fully informed choice on their future career.
> 3. Discuss equal opportunities and problems facing women and black people at work (e.g. sexual and racial harassment) as part of work experience preparation and debriefing.
> 4. Provide students with support, particularly women in traditional male areas of work.
> 5. Take seriously any complaints made by students and follow up with appropriate action.

Negotiating Placements with Employers

In negotiating work experience programmes with employers, staff should:

1. Ensure that all employers are aware of the College's Equal Opportunities Policies at an early state in negotiations and should discuss the issues raised by them from the Equal Opportunities Statement for Employers.
2. Be aware of the Sex Discrimination Act and which occupations are exempted and discuss with/challenge employers' claims to exemption where appropriate (advice is available from the Equal Opportunities Gender Co-ordinator on the Sex Discrimination Act and genuine occupational qualifications).
3. Monitor all placements prior to and during work experience to ensure that the College's Equal Opportunities Policies are being observed.

(Southwark College, November 1988)

In the light of the school or college policy, those involved in finding and supporting work experience placements need to agree how to deal with situations of discrimination when they face them. These situations may arise either at the stage of finding placements or when students are on placements and find themselves the object of, for example, racial or sexual harassment.

The Law, Equal Opportunities and Work Experience

In 1987 a judgement was given that a Croydon firm had contravened the Race Relations Act by refusing work experience placements to two pupils of West Indian origin. Both the Commission for Racial Equality and the Equal Opportunities Commission have since stated that a school/college could also face prosecution if they knowingly placed a student in a firm that practised such discrimination.

Equal Opportunities and Students

Issues of equal opportunities should be discussed with students at each stage of work experience. Although these stages are covered in more detail in earlier chapters, a summary of the equal opportunities dimensions are given below:

1. Arranging Placements

Many students request placements which reflect traditional choices within their family and community circle, yet other choices need to be available and young people encouraged to explore options outside a traditional range.

2. Activities and Strategies

(a) Some schools/colleges offer more than one period of work experience and encourage students to try as one of the options an area of work which is non-traditional but where they have an interest. For girls this might be jobs that are traditionally seen as 'men's jobs'.

(b) Work simulation, work shadowing and taster courses offer alternative ways of students testing out areas of work outside those they would traditionally choose.

3. Preparation

(a) Students who choose non-traditional areas of work need help in addressing sexism they might meet on placement. Discussions about attitudes, sessions on assertiveness-training and role-playing possible encounters can be useful ways of helping all students to prepare to face difficulties.

(b) Even students in traditional placements may meet racial or sexual harassment for which they need to be prepared. Again, discussion, assertiveness-training and role-play can prepare the students to face such situations and indicate to them the willingness of the teacher to take such issues seriously.

4. Support during Work Experience

(a) Teachers involved in placement visits can discuss how a student might raise an issue with an employer if she or he experiences racial or sexual harassment, or other discrimination.

(b) Teachers who have placed young women in non-traditional jobs must discuss openly with the employer what kind of support should be available both to the student and to the workers, who may find the situation uncomfortable. The decision in the Croydon case makes it clear that the employer has a responsibility not only to have an equal opportunities policy but to educate the staff in its implementation.

It also helps to work closely with the employer in developing the placement programme, as an employer may have the goodwill to offer a non-traditional placement yet not quite know how to make it work for the student.

5. Evaluation, Placement Maintenance and Development

(a) In order to ensure that employers continue to offer placements in non-traditional areas, particular care must be given in placement evaluation to what has been learned from the experience on all sides and to what might need improving for the future.

(b) Assignments to be used in preparing future students for placement may be developed from the experience of such a placement and with the co-operation of the placement provider.

(c) In any placement where students have experienced racial or sexual harassment or discrimination, the visiting tutor or work experience co-ordinator will need to raise this with the placement provider, discussing areas for development or making it clear that the placement offer cannot be accepted again.

In all such apparently difficult experiences, it is important in the first instance for the work experience tutor to see the employer's situation as an example of a 'training need'. The employer may lack the knowledge, information, awareness or understanding to do the 'right thing'. Tact in negotiation to a positive objective is an essential skill in the pioneering phase of developing equal opportunities principles and practices in firms and businesses where nothing much has previously been done. When the tutor's best efforts come to nought, then that placement is crossed off.

4. Designing Your Scheme

This chapter is about designing work experience programmes to match course content and individual student needs. It looks at the length of work experience placements, their timing in the course and institutional calendar, and the range of models available.

Allocating Time to Work Experience

The appropriate amount of work experience is that which best fits in with the pattern of the course as a whole. In some cases, Youth Training for example, this time may be specified and the course pattern may be developed accordingly. Such courses are usually centred around work placements complemented by an off-the-job training programme. In schools and in many colleges, work experience is just one of a range of contexts provided for students' learning. Used imaginatively, work experience is an interesting, adult and motivating setting within which students can pursue diverse goals, e.g.

- a learning base for GCSE;
- case study material for pre-vocational preparation courses;
- direct occupational training for Youth Training;
- vocational exploration and core skill implementation in CPVE, TVEI.

The amount of time allotted to work experience will depend on the degree to which it is a major context for the achievement of students' learning goals. In making this judgement, course and curriculum planners need to consider how work experience can be integrated into the overall scheme of work. The more successfully the work experience programme is integrated, the more not only students but also parents and staff will be able to see its relevance. This may allay common fears that time spent away from the classroom reduces chances of examination success.

Timing of Work Experience Placements

Once the amount of time is decided, the question arises of how to use that time. The aim of work experience on a particular course will suggest the appropriate timing for placements and the best model. Staff need to decide at what point during the particular course/student year work experience is most appropriate. For example,

- Is work experience to be used at the beginning of a course to provide stimulus material for future studies?
- Is work experience needed at the midway point in the course to try out skills learned and confidence acquired?
- Is work experience to be a regular integrated feature of the weekly timetable?
- Would work experience be most useful towards the end of a course, as a course goal to prepare students for transition into a work environment?
- Will work experience be organised in blocks or as a weekly, fortnightly, or monthly item on the timetable?

Avoid inadvertently building in difficulties. In deciding on the right model, be alert for clashes with other events in the curriculum calendar, such as residentials, mock examinations, subject choice evenings, sports days and bank holidays.

Style

The main preferred models for placements are listed below.

Model	Possibilities	Pitfalls
short block placements (1–3 weeks at appropriate points in course)	give young people time to settle into a working environment	present difficulties for all if a placement is not going well
	provide enough time for students to attempt interesting tasks and to begin to gain some occupational skills	may lead to restlessness on return to routine of school/college work
	offer enough time for students to make working relationships with employees, to feel relaxed and confident	require careful planning by whole course team to ensure integration

weekly placements (½ or 1 day)	are easily timetabled for both student and teacher time	do not really provide the continuity necessary for developing relationships, skills and a realistic sense of the work environment
	are easily integrated into the whole pattern of a course	unless carefully planned by employer and teacher, can be boringly repetitive and fail to allow for progression to more complex tasks
	are a focus of interest and give young people a break from school/college routine allow time for problem-solving between placement days	as work experience becomes routine, enthusiasm sometimes dims

extended block placements (more than 3 weeks)	give opportunity for trainee/ student to develop vocational skills	clear monitoring and work-based assessment are vital: long block placements are excellent if well organized but a poor use of time if not
	for maximum value, require work sponsor, tutor and student to see student's experience as *developmental* from an *initial* phase where a great deal of training and support are necessary, to an *operational* phase where a student's knowledge and skills become increasingly valuable to the student and to the work sponsor	

Activities for the Teacher

The following activities will help you to come to some decisions regarding the design of your work experience scheme.

1. If you are designing a new work experience scheme, what are the advantages and disadvantages of each work experience model for your particular students?

(See pages 32, 33.)

If you are working on a scheme which has followed the same model for some years, use the evaluation chart below to check that the model you are using is still appropriate.

SCHEME EVALUATION CHART

Model	Advantages	Disadvantages
short block placement (1–3 weeks)		
weekly placement (½ or 1 day)		
extended block placement (more than 3 weeks)		

2. Complete the timetabling checklist of course/year events below to ensure that any work experience proposal will not clash with major items already timetabled. (You may discover that a clash is inevitable, but this list will enable you to be forewarned, and therefore to prepare students and colleagues for the consequences.)

TIMETABLING CHECKLIST

Timetabled Events	Dates Scheduled	Notes
Careers interviews		
School journey/residential		
Mock examinations		
Examinations		

Other school/college activities
   1.
 	
   2.
 	
   3.		

Other course activities, e.g.
   1. computer course
 	
   2. job search
 	
   3.		

External factors, e.g.
   1. firm's holidays
 	
   2. hours of work
 	
   3. pressure points:
      Christmas, sales,
      Bank holidays		

3(a) Review **Activities 1** and **2**, noting your conclusions.

(b) Identify and note any changes you will need to make to current practice as a result of your review, e.g. changing the placement model or dates.

(c) Agree on an action plan, identify who will do what, and who needs asking or notifying about any changes.

5. Resourcing Work Experience Programmes

... 'try not to become frustrated when the resources you need are not readily available ...'

Staff in schools and colleges will be familiar with the annual cycle of estimating the resources needed for the new academic year. It is important to ensure that the resource implications of work experience are clearly identified and communicated to those senior staff with the job of promoting resource claims and then allocating funds accordingly. The quality and effectiveness of a work experience programme will depend on its being seen as an important, integral curriculum component that must be given a high priority when resources are being allocated.

When estimating for work experience, outline for senior staff the more general curricular aims of the work experience programme, then give, as far as possible, accurate estimates of:

- teaching staff time;
- timetable time;
- placement monitoring and visit time;
- clerical/administrative support and backup time;
- travelling costs for staff and students;
- any specific costs for uniforms, protective clothing, specialist equipment, learning materials.

Given the comparative novelty of work experience elements in the curriculum, their resource estimates may turn out to be rather more complex than those of other, more familiar, time-honoured slots on the timetable.

How the resources, once allocated, will be managed on a day-to-day basis will need to be decided. The question of who, for example, will be authorized to dispense petty cash and sign cheques, needs to be resolved at a reasonable interval before the start of the scheme.

Activities for the Teacher

The following activities will help you to work out resources required and then to plan a proposal for your senior manager(s).

1. Use the chart below to work out the resources required for your work experience programme. (Draw your own column three; column three below is filled in as an example.)

ESTIMATING RESOURCES

Questions to ask	Points to consider	Notes on your work experience programme
TEACHER TIME Who will find the placements? How long will this take?	Time will be required for: • contacting possible placements • preliminary placement visits • working with work sponsors to design their work experience programmes.	*Activity* Two course groups finding 40 placements one day a week. *Staff* Suggest Mr Gillies finds all placements. *Hours* Need 4 hours per week – or at least 3 timetabled consecutively.
Who will prepare and brief students?	Learning materials will need designing, writing and producing for students and work sponsors.	*Staff* Ms Ellis will co-ordinate all staff involved via course team meetings and teaching time with students. *Hours* No additional.

Questions to ask	Points to consider	Notes on your work experience programme
Who will co-ordinate the work experience programme, visit and monitor placements?	How and by whom will records be kept – especially work-based assessments? Time will be needed to liaise with work sponsors, review student progress and integrate work experience into classroom-based activities. (Course team meeting can be used for this.)	Ms Ellis will visit students, using time already allotted. Ms Brown and Mr McLoughlin will require one additional hour per week to allow them to use their class time for visits and writing up assessments. *Hours* 1×2 staff $= 2$ hours per week.
TIMETABLED TIME How many hours on the students' weekly timetable will need to be allocated for work experience?	The answer to this question will depend on the model of work experience selected: if weekly, timetablers will need alerting well in advance.	*Hours* e.g. 1 day per week $= 6$ hours per student.
CLERICAL/ ADMINISTRATIVE BACKUP What clerical help will you require?	Number of contacts you will be making by letter. Initial contacts, follow-up letters, placement confirmation letters, letters to parents, also briefing notes for students, learning materials, staff instructions for visits, will all require typing, collating, addressing, distributing. A telephone will need someone always available to receive messages – especially during work experience programme. *N.B.* The telephone plays a very significant part in work experience organization: arranging placements, keeping in touch with students and employers, crisis management etc.	e.g. 120 mailshots to work up interest, 120 follow-up phonecalls, 40 placement confirmation letters, 40 letters to parents. Request clerical help – possibly Mr Dobson in General Office – for 2 half days per week to set up scheme and to be available to take telephone messages once scheme in progress. *Hours* 1 clerical $\times 2$ half days per week $= 1$ day per week. Estimated amount of telephone use needed per week.

Questions to ask	Points to consider	Notes on your work experience programme
What equipment will you need made available to you?	Use of typewriter, word processor, telephones, photocopying machines.	Negotiate use of model office facilities with Head of Business Studies as well as arranging access for clerical help from General Office. *Hours* ½ day per week in preparation + 1 day per week during work experience.
What office space do you need?	A small room with a phone, if available, makes organization much easier. It provides a base, and students, staff and employers know where you can be found.	Suggest we ask to use room 92 – could share it with Careers Officer if necessary. *Hours* Need full-time during preparation and placements.
FUNDING How much money will be needed for travelling expenses, postage?	Fares will be needed for students both visiting and attending their placements, and also for staff visiting them. In the case of student fares you often need to be in a position to give out this money in advance.	*Item* *Amount* Postage c. £50 Student travel (40 placements × 25 occasions @ approx. 50p) c. £500 Staff visits (2 per week × 2 staff) c. £200
How much money do you estimate you will want for learning materials and other costs, e.g. special clothing, students' meals?	Where free school dinners are an entitlement, students will need lunch money.	*Amount* c. £350 Have arranged vouchers to nearby schools, where possible.
Will some provision be needed for hospitality for visiting employers? e.g. a work experience student/employer reception.	If employers come into school, you want to be in a position to offer coffee, afternoon tea, maybe lunch. Many schools/ colleges like to organize functions either before work experience, to inform employers, or afterwards, to allow employers and students to see how much work experience has achieved.	We would have catering option students prepare a buffet for employers as part of final course assessment. Will need funding for this (not sure of amount – will discuss with catering staff).

2. After thinking through your ideas in **Activity 1**, this activity provides a format for presenting your proposal to the appropriate senior manager(s). Heads of department, deputy heads or vice principals prefer to have a *written proposal* to which they can make a considered response.

You may want to use this format or design your own, using this as a guideline for points to remember.

To:

Re: Work Experience for _____ (course)

From: _____ (team, individual)

We would like to include the opportunity for work experience in the curriculum for our students this year. The course document states

_____

_____

and we have further clarified our aims as _____

_____

_____

We are proposing to have work experience placements for _____
(*number of students*) on the pattern of _____ (*model you have selected: weekly, block, etc.*) on the following dates _____

We have already confirmed that these dates do not clash with mock examinations/examinations/school journey/residential/induction. (*In the case where they do clash, you may need to add,* We are proposing ____ .)

We would like to discuss the question of resources. Our preliminary thoughts about resources required are as follows:

STAFF TIME (*List tasks, amount of time each will take and, if possible, the way a particular staff member could be timetabled to meet this.*)

ADMINISTRATIVE RESOURCES (*Clerical staff needed; use of phones and message system, printing/photocopying etc., including either staff or machine time it will require or amount of money needed.*)

FUNDING (*Itemise travel expenses, funds for learning materials, etc.*)

SUPPORT AND STAFF DEVELOPMENT (*List staff development that may be necessary, as well as the support you are asking from senior staff.*)

ACTION (*Make it clear by when you need to start getting placements and preparing students, and by when you will need to have approval.*)

REQUEST Could you meet with us within the next ＿＿＿＿＿＿＿＿ to discuss our suggestions and for you to give us advice about preparing the formal proposal that is necessary?

6. Preparing for Work Experience

Preparing Students

Work placements form but one part of students' curriculum. It is their experience of the curriculum as a whole that will determine their ability to make full use of the work experience component. The curricular style which will best prepare students for work experience will have equipped them to be active, confident learners who can recognize opportunities for learning even in new and unfamiliar situations. They will know how and when to ask questions, how to make full use of a demonstration of a task, what to remember and how to remember effectively, how to solve problems, how to use fault-finding techniques, how to probe to increase understanding and how to assess their own progress and achievement. Above all they will have a sense of direction and feel in control of the situation.

Work experience is the focus of this particular book. However, the influence of the overall curriculum culture in preparing students to go on placements cannot be understated.

There are four key elements in the preparation of students for work experience. Although these may be done in the order shown, in practice teachers will probably move flexibly between them. The four elements of preparation are:
1. negotiating work experience;
2. negotiating the nature of the placement;
3. allocating placements;
4. preparing for placements.

1. Negotiating Work Experience

The way in which work experience is introduced to students will either develop or dampen their enthusiasm for the idea. It is up to teachers to 'sell' work experience imaginatively and to present it as a challenge.

Suggested below are some launch point activities which have worked well in practice:

Activities to Set a Positive Tone
- Use slides or a video showing past years' placements.
- Explain via quotes and case studies how work experience has benefited other students.

- Describe, with examples, how students have used work experience to produce evidence of learning for profiles and portfolios.
- Invite students who have already been on work experience to talk with the group.

Activities for Exploring Prior Knowlege of Work and the Workplace and to Gauge a Student's Initial Reaction to Work Experience

- Give out a questionnaire (example below). Ask each student to fill this in alone without any discussion.

The questionnaire then becomes the basis for small group discussions. Each small group puts their ideas on a flipchart and gives feedback to the whole group. A list of group concerns can then be compiled to be dealt with immediately or later as appropriate.

Questionnaire

1. What do you know about work experience?
   a lot   a bit   very little   nothing at all

2. Do you know anyone who has been on work experience?
   Yes   no

3. If you answered yes to number 2, what did he/she think of it?
   in favour   not in favour

4. How do you feel about going on work experience?
(Tick as many statements as apply to you)

pleased ☐

excited ☐

keen but scared ☐

think it will be a good opportunity to learn ☐

think it is a good idea ☐

think it is a waste of time ☐

scared ☐

would rather stay in school/college ☐

don't want to go ☐

don't mind one way or the other ☐

5. Off the top of your head, what sort of placements do you think:
would interest you most? _____
would interest you least? _____

- Have a question and answer session. Give students time to prepare their questions alone or in pairs and then put them to you.

The teacher must undertake to answer as fully and honestly as possible. Students may want answers to questions such as:

When will we be going on work experience? ☐

When will I know where I am going? ☐

Can I choose where to go? ☐

If I have a Saturday job, do I still have to go? ☐

Can two of us go to the same place? ☐

Will I be able to leave in time to

    (a) get to my evening job, or ☐

    (b) pick up my little sister after school? ☐

Will it count towards my certificate? ☐

What if I don't get on or can't do things? ☐

How long will the placement last? ☐

What is the point when there are no jobs anyway? ☐

The questions students ask initially might not at first lead to any detailed discussion of work experience. However, it is important that teachers listen and respond, whatever the level of questioning. This is the beginning of students' own exploration of work experience. They can understand in greater depth only when they have actually been on placement.

2. Negotiating the Nature of the Placement

Once the topic of work experience has been raised, students will want to discuss their own particular needs and their expectations of what going on placement entails.

Teachers will probably have a picture of the kind of placement that will best suit each of their students. Students themselves will have ideas about what they want, or possibly what they don't want, in a placement. Work experience stands a much better chance of success if teachers and students spend time sharing these ideas and expectations.

Some questions that might usefully be put to students are:

What age of person would you most like to work with?
What size of organization would you prefer?

What distance from your home are you willing to travel?

What previous jobs or placements have you done? What did you do and for how long?

Do you prefer working on your own, in a small group, or with a lot of people?

What kind of placement do you think would suit you best? For example, indoor or outdoor; office work or manual work; where you have to wear a suit or a uniform; working shift hours or regular hours; with the public or with machines?

What expectations do your parents have? For example, do they think certain jobs are unsuitable for girls/boys? Do they want you to be something in particular? Would they totally disapprove of some jobs?

What jobs do you think are most prestigious? What jobs would you refuse even to consider?

Are there any jobs you think are unsuitable for girls/boys, and why?

There are a variety of ways in which you might want to use these questions. For example, in a questionnaire, as a kind of card game, with students interviewing each other, with individual student interviews.

3. Allocating Placements

Do not make the mistake of seeing placement allocation as a routine part of the administration of work experience. Work experience becomes a more interesting prospect once students are involved in the practical possibilities. The more students are involved in placement allocation, the more likely they are to get the maximum benefit from work experience. Allocating placements is an excellent opportunity for involving them in making decisions.

There are a variety of ways of allocating placements, several of which are listed below. Points to consider before deciding on a method include: the aim of the scheme, placements available, requirements and expectations of employers, the level of self-confidence and self-awareness both of individual students and of the student group, and the level of confidence staff have about involving students in the decision-making process. Any course specifications which might affect placements must also be taken into account.

Consider the models below, weighing up the advantages and disadvantages before making a choice.

Model	Method
Placements primarily assigned by teacher	Teacher allocates placements after general discussion with individual students.
Students select preferred area for their placement.	Students identify the area of work they would prefer for work experience (using activities and exercises such as those at the end of this chapter) then teacher assigns specific placement
Students negotiate their own placement	Details of placements are put on display, perhaps as part of a mock job centre, and students select and negotiate their placement with the teacher.
Teacher and student group work together to assign placements	Course group and teacher discuss all placements and all students, and assign placements by consensus.
Students assist teacher in finding placements	Students are asked to look in their neighbourhoods and talk to parents and friends to find placements for themselves and/or other students. (This method can be incorporated into any of the above models.)

4. Preparing for the Placement

Once each student has a definite work experience placement, there are three stages in preparing for that placement:

1. Introducing students to their placements
– introducing the programme
– visiting the placement
2. Pre-placement briefing and confidence building
3. Last minute reminders.

It is advisable not to leave out or skip over any of these stages. Teachers have observed that students raise different concerns at different stages, and that they need the same information repeated frequently in the period leading up to work experience.

It will take at least one session, and preferably more, to cover each stage of preparation. The outlines of sessions and assignments on which teachers can build to meet the specific requirements of their student group are presented in the next chapter. They are based on the practice of experienced work experience tutors.

7. Student Assignments

... 'ensure adequate safety precautions are taken...'

1. Introducing Students to their Placement

Aim

Students should visit and find out as much as possible about their work placement prior to the commencement of work experience. This assignment is about preparing for, planning and going on this fact-finding visit. The more students undertake the arrangements themselves, the more involved in and committed to work experience they will become.

Task 1. Arranging the Visit

This might involve:
- checking name of firm, contact person, address;
- writing or phoning to make arrangements for the visit and asking for directions;
- writing to confirm arrangements;
- notifying teacher of arrangements.

Task 2. Planning the Journey

Planning might involve:
- locating the place on the map;
- identifying the route and public transport;
- clarifying the amount of time it will take;
- making sure of the fare required;

Task 3. Giving and Getting Information

Preparation for talking to the placement provider might include group activities such as:

- practice in asking questions to get the fullest possible answers;
- thinking out what questions the placement provider might ask and practising answering them, e.g. through role-play with a partner or in a group, taking it in turns to ask each member relevant and 'awkward' questions.

Task 4. The Visit

This might involve:
- keeping notes;
- taking a picture of the placement (if cameras are available) or making a sketch;
- getting any promotional literature the firm has, to show to the rest of the group and to read in preparation for the placement.

2. Preparing the Student Group for Work Experience

Aim

Students will have worked with each other for part of a year or longer, and separating for work experience can be very unsettling, reminding them, as it will, that their time together is limited. The following tasks are designed to help them use this reality constructively and to support each other through it.

Task 1. Presentations

Following the pre-placement visits students prepare and give presentations on what they know about their placements to date and their first impressions. It will be useful to keep some record of these to compare with impressions after time spent in the placements.

Task 2. Questions on Presentations

When listening to each presentation, others in the group should note questions to ask and identify any gaps in the information given.

Task 3. Discussion on Visits

Discussion groups compare notes about the visits, spotting differences and similarities in placement impressions, and feelings about meeting new people.

Task 4. Locating Placements

Make or mount a large map of the locality covered by all the placements. Each student should pin in the appropriate place the name of their placement and the picture or photograph if they have made such a record.

Task 5. Familiarization with Placements

In groups of three visit each student's placement location, only calling in if this has been pre-arranged with the placement provider.
or
With the entire group, drive around in a mini-bus to see where the students will be. Each student in turn should give directions to his/her location, using a map.

3. Health and Safety in the Workplace

Aim

It is the primary responsibility of teachers to prepare students going on placement to be conscious of health and safety issues. Whilst on placement, health and safety will be the responsibility of the placement provider. This assignment introduces students to health and safety issues and how to deal with health and safety situations on work experience.

Task 1. Raising Awareness of Health and Safety

In order to raise students' awareness of health and safety issues, the following approaches may be used:
- watching health and safety videos;
- inviting a speaker from the Health and Safety Executive or a trade union health and safety officer;
- using slides and pictures of previous work experience placements to get students to identify health and safety issues in different work

settings, drawing out points about safety for students and other workers and, if applicable, for the general public and consumers.

The discussion should help students clarify their own responsibility and that of the tutor and of the placement providers for health and safety issues during work experience.

Task 2. Points to Check

Ask students to draw up a list of health and safety points to check at their placements, discussing how to deal with situations which they observe on their preliminary visit to be not in accord with health and safety regulations, e.g. workers on a building site choosing not to wear hard hats.

Task 3. Discussion and Role-play

Discuss and role-play how students should handle a situation during work experience when health and safety regulations are being contravened, knowing when to raise the issue with the employer and when to notify the tutor, e.g:

- being asked to do something they know is unsafe;
- working with someone who is doing something unsafe which could endanger them;
- wanting to comply with health and safety regulations, e.g. wearing a protective helmet provided, but finding that none of the workers are doing so and are dismissive about the need to do so.

4. Dressing for the Part

Aim

The transition from school or college to work experience may mean students making changes in how they present themselves. The aim of these activities is to give students the opportunity to discuss the appropriate 'image' and dress for different kinds of work.

Task 1. Identifying Appropriate Dress

Ask students to make and complete a chart similar to the one below, listing their own proposed placements and information they have about required dress.

Placements (list each in group)	Image they are trying to create	Safety points	Appropriate dress
Right Now Hairdressing (in the salon)	Fashionable, affluent	Shoes suitable for standing; clothes that can stand being splashed with water, lotions.	Comfortable clothing that looks like high street fashion.
TWL Engineering (factory floor)		Shoes with toes well protected; hair up, if long; no loose clothing or jewellery.	Heavy shoes, tough trousers/jeans
M and G department store (shelf-filler)		Hair clean and tidy for hygiene; nails clean and trimmed; comfortable shoes for standing.	Uniform provided; low shoes, no coloured tights or outrageous make-up.

Task 2. Choosing your Image

Using the chart from Task 1 as the basis, encourage students to discuss the kind of image they wish to present.

Task 3. Searching your Wardrobe

Encourage students to identify what they have that is appropriate to wear and what they need. The teacher will need to know what grants may be available to the course and/or to individuals for safety clothing. The work placement provider is normally expected to provide any special clothing and/or equipment.

5. Roles and Relationships

Aim

Students need to be aware that the success of work experience will depend not only on doing tasks well but also on getting on with the people. They may need to learn and rehearse skills to deal with problems or misunderstandings that arise.

Task 1. Dealing with People at Work

Give the students the opportunity to discuss how they would handle some of the most common situations which arise during placements. It is useful to have a selection of situations to use as the focus for discussions. These can be 'mini-dramas' recorded by last year's students or ones written by this year's students.

(a) Divide students into groups of three and give them a ten-line 'mini-drama' to prepare for presentation to the whole group. Each group can present their 'mini-drama' and the teacher will use it to draw out the discussion about various approaches to the issues raised.

(b) Each group of three students can be given a last line and asked to construct a mini-drama of no more than ten lines and present it to the whole group for discussion. Some possible last lines might be:

– I don't care; keep your hands to yourself.

– I'm glad I asked you. I understand much better now.

– Well, if that's how you feel you can just go back to college right now.

– YOU DID WHAT?

– You're a racist, that's what you are!

– That's okay. Give it another try.

Task 2. Dealing with Misunderstanding and Conflict

It can be helpful to draw up some 'ground-rules' about how to handle misunderstandings and conflict during the placement to give students the opportunity to rehearse how they and their tutor would handle various situations. This can give students a way of judging their own behaviour and understanding others, and will help them know what role the college or school tutor plays during the placement.

Divide students into groups of three, giving each group the same topic and scenario to rehearse, then bring the groups together to discuss and draw out some ground-rules for behaviour. Finally students return to their groups to re-play the scene according to the ground-rules they have just established. Students should play the work experience tutor, the student on placement, and the placement supervisor or another employee.

It can be helpful if the teacher chooses illustrations from the experience of former students, around areas such as:

(a) Asking for something, e.g. directions to the loo, or how to do something.
(b) Coping with anger, their own and others.
(c) Accepting criticism, e.g. when they have made a mistake or been late.
(d) Giving and receiving compliments, e.g. thanking or being thanked.

The framework of assertiveness-training can be helpful in giving students a common language by which they can identify behaviour that is aggressive, passive or assertive, and rehearse some of the basic points such as:

- putting their own point of view *and* trying to listen to the other side;
- being very specific when they want to say something, e.g. 'I am fed up being the only one who makes tea', not 'I hate it here';
- stating clearly what they are asking, introducing it with 'I', e.g. 'I would like to have experience doing something besides addressing envelopes' rather than 'You're treating me like a slave'.

Task 3. Carrying on a Conversation at Work

Many young people find it difficult to carry on conversations with older workmates. Rehearsal in talking with other people and asking them questions can help them to feel more at ease. Ask everyone in the group to listen to the same television programme or watch the news or bring in a newspaper. Get them to talk in pairs about something they have seen or read, and in the whole group look at issues such as:

- what you do if you are not interested in/don't know about something;
- what is an appropriate greeting when you get to work;
- how you deal with jokes you feel are offensive.

Task 4. Roles and Titles

Many teachers prefer to be called by their first names these days and have an informal relationship with their students. This is true for some employers but not for others. Discussion and/or rehearsal can help students explore the differences in roles and titles.

Task 5. Rehearsing for Placement Visits

Where possible it is important for all students to meet the tutor who will visit them during the placement and clarify the point of those visits. If a group is comfortable with role-play, it can also be helpful to rehearse (a) a visit that goes wrong (e.g. by the tutor 'showing the student up' or the tutor and employer talking over the student's head) and (b) a visit which is supportive and informative.

Use any materials that the employer will have for assessment, and give the students an opportunity to become familiar with these and their purpose.

6. Final Briefing

Aim

The aim of the following tasks is to cover the final points students need to be clear about in the week or so before work experience begins.

Task 1. Knowing it All

Students will need to have certain information and material for work experience. Prepare a checklist and ask each student to do a final check that they have all the information they require.

- practical information such as:
  - name and address of placement
  - phone number of placement and college
  - directions
  - expenses sheets.

- material such as:
  - copy of programme
  - any work assignments
  - diary and log book, if required.

Task 2. Timekeeping and Absence

Many students run into difficulties not only in being late or absent but in not knowing the appropriate way to handle such a situation. It may be useful to clarify what the school or college expects from the student, what the employer expects, and what are the consequences of repeated absence or lateness.

Task 3. Dealing with Anxieties

It can be helpful to discuss again the reasons for work experience and the expectations students have, giving them a last-minute opportunity to voice any anxieties. A teacher may find it useful to offer a few minutes' time to each student individually so as to make sure there are no difficulties that might stand in their way.

Task 4. Getting There

Depending on the group and the individuals, it may be helpful to arrange to accompany some students to the placement on the first morning or to meet them during their lunch hour. Ask all students to share what preparations they have made for getting up on time and getting through the first day.

8. Working with Colleagues and Placement Providers

A work experience programme depends for its success on a sound partnership between school/college and local employers. This is best achieved by teachers establishing a personal contact with the responsible person in a local firm or organization. The aim is to develop a good working relationship from the very first encounter. This relationship works best when both parties understand and value each other's contribution to the scheme.

It is also important, especially to local business people, that work experience is clearly seen to be under the leadership of a senior figure on the staff of the school or college. Often a preliminary meeting which combines a formal briefing with a small social occasion can effectively launch the scheme. The extent to which senior staff are present and seen to be committed to work experience will be taken by local industry and commerce as one significant indicator of the value given to the scheme by the school/college.

Prejudices and stereotypical views of each other abound amongst teachers and employers. These are fed by stories of bad placements on the one side and poorly prepared students on the other. Many teachers are surprised to discover how much goodwill exists amongst employers towards young people. Equally, many employers are surprised at the interest teachers show in their work and at the breadth of the curriculum being followed in schools and colleges.

This chapter looks at ways teachers and employers can work together through the various stages of work experience preparation to ensure a well-planned, high-quality placement for each student. These stages are:

1. Finding placements;

2. Briefing the placement finder(s);

3. Putting questions to the work sponsors;

4. Giving information to the work sponsors;

5. Planning the placement programme.

1. Finding Placements

Selling work experience to potential sponsors requires enthusiasm and perseverance. Personal contact, whether by letter or telephone, or by calling in person, is more effective than impersonal, blanket mailings. It is best to contact large organizations by phone or letter before any visit but, with small local firms, a 'drop-in' visit may be acceptable if it is well-timed, i.e. not during their busiest period.

Those involved in work experience should always be on the lookout for introductions and leads about placements, e.g.

- through students and their parents;
- through friends and colleagues;
- from school and college governors and the PTA;
- from the Careers Office and/or the school/college industry co-ordinators;
- from the local businesses, community, arts and charitable organizations.

2. Briefing the Placement Finder(s)

Anyone finding placements for work experience needs a system for recording information, clear guidelines about the requirements of the particular course, and contact with the individual students and placement providers.

In cases where it is the course tutor who is finding placements, the lines of contact are clear. Where a person outside the staff or course team is finding placements or where more than one member of the teaching team is involved, clear briefing at each of these points is essential.

In colleges or schools where banks of placement-offers are collected without reference to individual students or courses, the placement provider will need to develop a more specific programme for each student coming on work experience.

Whoever finds the placements, keeping records of every contact and conversation is *essential*. Few things diminish the credibility of a work experience scheme more than two teachers phoning the same employer.

Teachers design work experience record-keeping systems to suit their own circumstances. Whatever the system, it should give the following information:

- Places contacted and result of those contacts (whether yes or no) for present use and future information;

- Placements agreed: name of contact person, dates they can take someone and how many students they can take for each time period.

Every phone call and letter about work experience should be recorded and filed. There is no point in losing employer goodwill through careless administration.

Placement finders should always:

- *State clearly* the aims of the work experience, how long it lasts, and the dates when placements are needed;
- *Follow up* any contact – a letter with a call, or a call with a letter;
- *Note* every conversation, or letter, however brief or informal.

3. Putting Questions to Potential Work Sponsors

When establishing a bank of reliable information about potential work placement providers, a standard checklist of questions is helpful. It is easy to forget questions in the course of a conversation, and essential facts can be missed.

The answers establish a basis from which to plan a placement programme. The placement profile that results should give as detailed a picture as possible to assist in choosing the right placement for each student.

Listed below are some useful guidelines:

General Information

- What are the address and telephone number of the company?
- What is the name of the work experience contact?
- What is the work of the organization?
- How many people are employed?
- How long has work experience been offered?
- How are the health and safety of employees ensured?

Placement Opportunities

- What range of placement opportunities can be offered and what tasks are required within each one?
- What skills will students require for the various placements?
- Are there placement opportunities for students with a handicap? Does the firm have a ramp for wheelchair access, lifts, audio-enhanced phones for those with partial hearing?

- Would the work adversely affect or be unsuitable for students with certain health conditions, such as epilepsy, asthma, colour blindness?

Placement Arrangements

- What hours are proposed?
- What are the arrangements for lunch breaks?
- What is expected with regard to dress-style, protective clothing? Will the employer provide safety clothing or a uniform?
- What are the arrangements for:
  - introducing the student to the placement and placement provider?
  - letting the student phone to arrange a visit in advance of starting?
  - letting the student visit for an initial informal meeting?
  - teacher visits during work experience?
- Will the employer/work sponsor visit the college or school?

Placement Contacts

- Who will the student's immediate supervisor be?
- Whom should the student or teacher phone in case of illness or lateness?

4. Giving Information to Work Sponsors

The rules and culture of school or college may be unfamiliar to a work sponsor. In order to plan placements, work placement providers need information from teachers.

Work placement providers have businesses to run, and providing work experience is only a small part of their activities. It will help if they are given accurate and comprehensive guidelines about work experience.

Some useful points of information include:

- the aims of the work experience programme;
- the nature of the course of which work experience is a part, e.g. TVEI, CPVE, GCSE, BTEC, SCOTVEC;
- the kind of work students are doing at college or school. Both a course curriculum and examples of students' written and practical

work can help in more accurately gauging the right placement programme to provide;

- the scheme arrangements, e.g.
  - any statutory regulations, such as health and safety requirements
  - insurance, third party liability
  - whom to contact at school/college and the system for leaving messages
  - finances: clarify whether students get fares, free lunches, coffee/tea
  - plans for finalizing the programme, visits by teachers, and assessment of student progress/achievement.

Introducing the young person to the placement and to their work sponsor is important. Potential work sponsors should be informed when placements will be allocated, whether the placement provider will be involved in allocating placements, and how their student will be introduced to them.

5. Planning the Placement Programme

Once a placement is provisionally agreed the next steps are:

(a) working out practical arrangements
(b) planning the placement programme.

Working out Practical Arrangements

Together the tutor or placement finder and the placement provider agree approaches on the following:

Points to raise	Some options
Arrangements for an introductory meeting between student(s) and placement provider.	• Student will write/ring to arrange visit to the workplace. • Teacher will write/ring to arrange visit for student to the workplace. • Placement provider will visit the school to meet the student and find out about the course.
Responsibility for special requirements for placement, e.g. clothing, headgear.	• Placement provider will furnish all necessary clothing and equipment. • School/college will provide the student with necessary clothing and equipment.
Provision of fares, tea, coffee, lunch, other expenses incurred.	• Placement provider will fund. • School/college will fund. • Funding shared by agreement. • Student will meet own expenses for meals and school/college will pay travel expenses.
Teacher visits to students on placement – the purpose of the visits and the most convenient times in the week for the work placement provider.	• Dates for visits are agreed in advance. • System for teachers to arrange visits is agreed. • 'Agenda' for visits is agreed, i.e. a time for the teacher to talk with the student, with the employer, and for teacher, student and employer to talk together.
Assessing students' progress and achievement.	• Asking the work placement providers to assess students' performance against a competence checklist and to involve students actively in the assessment process.

Points to raise	Some options
	• Explaining that the teacher will, with the placement provider and the student, review a student's progress and record his/her achievement when visiting the placement.
Establishing a procedure for dealing with problems that might arise during a placement.	• Placement providers are given a telephone number to ring in case of difficulty and the work experience backup system provided by the college/school is fully explained.
	• Agree that a meeting will be held involving teacher, placement provider and student to try to reach an acceptable solution to a problem before a placement is deemed to be unworkable.

Planning a Placement Programme

The first stage of planning a programme for the individual student on placement is to identify the broad areas of experience that a particular work placement offers. Within each of these broad areas will be specific tasks. An analysis of these will give a picture of the range of skills and knowledge a student will be able to learn and practice within the placement. Once these areas and tasks are identified, a programme can be drawn up showing in as much detail as is practically possible exactly what the student will be doing throughout the placement, where he/she will be working (if he/she is to move between departments or sites) and when he/she can expect to be doing each of the tasks.

Activities for the Teacher

1. Draft a letter to send to potential placement providers.
   - State clearly who you are and what you want.
   - Explain the purpose of work experience.
   - Give brief details of the course your students are following.
   - State that you will ring within the next week to see if they will be able to help.

2. Prepare exactly what you will say if you:
   (a) canvass for your placements by phone;
   (b) follow up an initial letter with a phone call.

If possible rehearse your approach with a colleague: it is surprisingly difficult to give clear and concise information on the telephone and to ask for placements from people you have never met.

3. Construct your own system for recording information as a basis for a placement bank.

4. Design an information sheet or leaflet explaining to employers the role of the work experience provider. Include details of exactly what is expected and a clear statement about assessment.

9. Supporting Work Experience

... 'try and give support to the more nervous pupil on their first day ...'

While students are on placement the school/college remains responsible for their welfare and progress. Once placements begin, however, the day-to-day management of students' activities shifts from teachers to the work placement providers.

Teachers will want to give maximum support to the work placement providers without interfering unnecessarily. Equally they will want to keep in contact with their students without appearing to be constantly checking on them.

Some ways to strike the right balance and give appropriate back-up are suggested in this chapter.

1. Provision of an Effective Communication System

From the start of work experience placements, school/college could provide a 'phone-in' facility for both students and work placement providers so that a speedy response can be made to queries and problems. This will require an extension, answered promptly during work experience hours, and a message-taking service that contacts the relevant teacher quickly.

This service will work more efficiently if the school/college switchboard and office staff have been properly briefed about work experience. A short training session for office staff to explain work experience and highlight the importance of prompt action on telephone calls received helps ensure that office staff feel well-informed and involved in working for the success of the scheme.

A work experience information bulletin will keep the switchboard, the general office and all teaching staff informed. Copies placed by the telephone in the staff room and at other key points will give staff easy access to up-to-date information. The contents might include:

Work Experience Information Bulletin

Index

- Details of the work experience scheme

- Names and timetables of staff organizing the scheme

- Questions to put to callers if none of the staff responsible for the scheme can be found

- Quick reference list of students on placement

- Full list of students on placement with details of the placements and placement contact person

- Procedure for taking and quickly passing on in-coming messages

---

2. Support Facilities for Students

Students on placement must get on as adults in the adult world of work. Sensitive teachers will make sure that they do nothing to undermine their students developing feelings of maturity and self-reliance. At the same time they will want to make sure students feel confident that teachers are still there, interested in what they are doing, and available to help if necessary. Suggested student support facilities are:

- pre-arranged support for any student with a particularly bad attack of first-day nerves, e.g. student accompanied by a teacher on the first morning; a first-day phone call; meeting for lunch; a visit to school/college to see a teacher at the end of the day;

- regular tutor visits to placements;
- students knowing how to get in touch with their tutor quickly in case of difficulties.

During their preparation for work experience, students will have been encouraged to feel positive about their achievements on placement and not to see mistakes as failures. This perspective will need reinforcement during placements. Few students go through a placement without some ups and downs. A positive attitude to difficulties may enable a student to persevere rather than abandon work experience. Examples of potential difficulties and possible solutions are described in Chapter 11. There will, however, be students who will be unable to complete a placement. In such instances, alternative arrangements, usually not another placement, must be made.

3. Support of Work Placement Providers

Teachers can support the placement providers in four main ways:

- by effective communication;
- by providing clear instructions for the use of the documentation for on-going assessment of students' achievements and progress;
- by openly showing appreciation of efforts made by placement providers and, if difficulties do arise, by emphasizing that this is not necessarily a failure on anybody's part;
- by making the facilities of the school available to the work placement provider. Just as teachers can learn on visits to employers' premises, so placement providers might welcome a day back in school/college for themselves or their staff, e.g. in the computer room to learn how to do spreadsheets, or in classes to see what schools are like now. Perhaps the student on placement could act as a host/guide for such a visit.

4. Support of Teacher Colleagues

The teachers who will visit students on placement may not all have been closely involved in organizing and preparing for work experience. Many teachers are unfamiliar with workplaces outside school/college and feel rather unsure as to what is expected of them. Teachers responsible for organizing work experience can help allay any fears by the provision of guidelines and briefing notes.

It is worth pointing out to staff that whilst the chief purpose of visits is to support students and then placement providers, the visits can also provide staff themselves with a useful opportunity to develop, e.g. updating their own industrial or commercial knowledge, or gathering material on which to base assignments and case studies.

Activities for the Teacher

1. Design your own work experience bulletin. As a guide use the sample index for a work experience bulletin on page 67.

2. Ask the person responsible for INSET/staff development to arrange a session for staff on supporting work experience. The aims of this session might be to brief staff on the purpose and aims of work experience and to prepare them for their role as placement visitors.

10. Work Placement Visits by Teachers

Work placement visits are the main link between the school/college and work placement providers during work experience. They are the focus of personal contact between teachers and their students on placement. A co-ordinated programme of visits to each placement helps ensure the success of work experience and facilitates the integration of work experience with other elements of the curriculum.

A great deal of class contact time is released during work placements. This time should be timetabled for work experience visits. A rota is then drawn up by the work experience organizers and implemented by a senior member of staff. In the past, work experience organizers have fallen into the trap of regarding work experience visiting as an optional staff activity. The result has been that the bulk of the visiting has been done by a few people. It is far better to formalize the arrangements. Visits should be allocated in direct correlation to the amount of class contact time released by work experience in a teacher's timetable.

Which teacher will visit which placement can be decided by:

- staff choosing which students they will visit;
- students requesting visits from particular tutors;
- course team discussion;
- the work experience co-ordinator assigning placement visits.

The following information will need to be recorded for each teacher who is undertaking placement visits:

- number of teaching hours released by work experience;
- method of transport, e.g. own car, public transport;
- home address, for the possibility of making visits near to home;
- specialist teaching area;
- special requests/considerations regarding placement visits.

It is best if tutors know, and preferably teach, the students they will visit. It is also helpful to the students if they know which teacher they may expect to visit them before they go on their placements.

Each teacher visiting placements will need written details of the student(s) they are to visit: names, addresses, telephone numbers; names of staff contacts in the placements; details of travelling directions; and any special instructions for the visit.

It is useful to have an overall picture of how the schedule of visits is progressing. One way of doing this is by a visit chart on the wall of the staff room or work experience base, giving details of all visits planned and completed. No student must be overlooked. A careful check must be kept by the teachers responsible for the scheme to see that visits do happen.

Guidelines for Teacher Visits to Placements

Work experience organizers can give teachers a placement visit pack containing some helpful notes on their role, together with copies of any forms they are to complete during or after the visit. The pack might include:

1. Information on Procedures

- Ring up first and make an appointment with the placement provider.
- Note the time and date of the visit on wall chart.
- Telephone in the morning or the day before to confirm the visit, in case either student or work sponsor is off work or the timing is inconvenient.

2. Approaches for Visiting

- Make the opportunity to talk to students on their own as well as with the placement provider so as to allow them to discuss any problems they may be experiencing.
- Check that the placement is interesting and enjoyable, that the student feels the programme is being followed and that he/she is gaining from the experience.
- Be careful not to speak about the student to the placement provider as if the student were not present, or vice versa.
- Be sensitive to the changed roles of teacher and student in the place of work: the teacher is the visitor, the student, with the placement provider, is the host.

3. Agenda with Placement Provider

- Review with the placement provider how the programme is developing. Check whether either the placement provider or the student feels any changes should be made.

• Discuss the assessment criteria for the placement, of which both student and placement provider will have copies. Review with them the student's learning to date and make sure that records are being kept.

• Make time with the placement provider, without the student, to make sure he/she understands the assessment documentation required.

4. Visiting Staff Brief

• Take the opportunity to look around the workplace. Arrange with the student and the work placement provider to be shown around.

• Be open about what you would like to know and learn, in order to keep up to date in this area of work.

• Complete the visit by filling in any record form immediately and returning it to the appropriate person.

Activities for the Teacher

1. Draw up your own guidelines for placement visitors based on the points mentioned in this chapter.

2. If possible, arrange a briefing session to ensure that all placement visitors are familiar with the guidelines, clear about the assessment work they need to do with the placement provider and student, and sensitive to the changed relationship with students on work experience.

3. Design a placement visit report form to ensure the information needed is obtained from the tutor placement visits.

11. Positive Problem Solving

'... try to prevent any breakdown in the pupil/employer relationship ...'

Be positive! Be constructive! Be realistic! If teachers can adopt this approach in helping students and placement providers work through difficulties and disagreements, then acceptable solutions can usually be found.

Problems as Learning Opportunities

Problems present an opportunity for learning and for personal development. Whilst preparing for work experience placements, students, teachers and work placement providers will have discussed the importance of learning from mistakes and sorting out misunderstandings. Sometimes, in making the transition from school to workplace, students take time to learn appropriate and expected behaviour. With a little goodwill from all concerned, the misunderstandings that arise can soon be sorted out.

Occasionally, problems of a more serious nature occur, e.g. a complete lack of co-operation from the student, continuing racist remarks from an employee. Such circumstances may lead to the ending of a particular placement. Where this happens, the teacher must make time to talk the situation through with the student and decide on the appropriate course of action.

A Creative Approach

Approaching *realistically* a situation such as the premature end of a placement can mean, for the teacher, recognizing that for this particular student there is no possibility of carrying on. Approaching it *positively*, instead of punitively, will enable teachers to help the student consider what he/she can learn from the experience.

Preparing for Problems

Teachers may find it useful, before placements begin, to work out the approach they will take in response to the different types of problems that may occur during the scheme. Although details will differ with each situation, prior thought about the general approach can help prevent a difficulty turning into a crisis. At the end of this chapter, some actual situations drawn from a range of work experience settings are offered for course team consideration.

Reaching a Solution

Whenever problems occur, it is best to solve them in such a way that no loose ends remain. The immediate response of a teacher may be to bring the student back to school or college while sorting things out. Even as a temporary measure this needs to be handled carefully, so that the student does not feel she or he has 'lost face' and cannot return to the placement.

In attempting to reach the best solution, teachers may find the following guidelines helpful.

- Hear all sides of the story.
- Manage the situation to give the student and the placement provider the opportunity to talk together and come up with their own solution.
- Be prepared, when necessary, to refer the problem to the head teacher or principal, particularly in areas that have legal and/or equal opportunities implications.
- Accept that withdrawal from the placement may be the best solution and, in such situations, make time to help the student come to terms with this decision.

A sensitive handling of the situation will give all of those involved, including the teacher, an opportunity to learn from what has happened.

Activities for the Teacher

Here are some typical problems you might face during work experience. They are presented in the form of telephone messages waiting for you in your in-tray.

The first message is presented as an example. The problem is clarified, then discussed in a course team meeting where strategies for tackling the problem are identified.

Working in a group or on your own, use the same format to think through how you might respond to each message. If you have already run a work experience scheme, use actual messages you have received or problems you have confronted. Discuss how you tackled the problems presented, and with what results.

1. 'John Pardoe of Erwax Engineering phoned to say that Patrick Wright had phoned to say he was ill both yesterday and today, and that he was late every day last week. Getting fed up. Please phone back immediately.'

(a) Clarify the problem

Phoned back John Pardoe immediately to ask for details of the situation. He says Patrick's lateness means that he is not following much of the agreed programme. He does no think there is any point in keeping Patrick for the last three days this week, since they find his attitude difficult. 'No initiative, just stands around after arriving late,' is how he described it. John would be willing to meet Patrick with me and talk to him about the firm's decision.

Rang Patrick at home and arranged for him to meet me at school the next day. He felt they 'got on his back' after he was late the first day, even though he explained he had taken the wrong bus. Agreed that he had not apologized for being late. He is also angry because, after that, they just had him making the tea. I also sensed that for all his posturing, he was quite nervous about being able to fit in, and cope with the work. Finally we agreed he would go with me to see the employer.

(b) Course Team Discussion

This is a summary of our discussion at the course team meeting:

The situation with work experience reflects Patrick's attitude in school as well: everyone is always 'on his back', as he sees it. He is consistently late to school, too, but had been adamant in our preparations for work experience that he would manage to be on time during his placement.

(c) Strategies for Tackling the Situation

After a full discussion we agreed the following plan of action:
   (i) Meeting with Patrick and placement provider. Tutor to encourage placement provider to be straight with Patrick about:
   – what it signalled to the firm when he was late the first day, came in surly, and did not even apologize;
   – what he could have done differently;
   – why they then treated him as they did.
   (ii) Meeting with Patrick and tutor in multi-skills workshop to design a two-day diagnostic programme so that he can test himself and feel he has achieved something from the work experience.
   (iii) Meeting with his visiting tutor to go through the assessment form and assess for himself what he has learned from the experience.
   (iv) Negotiation about another work experience placement later in the year.

2. 'Janis Freeman phoned to say she wasn't going back to work today. What she said that is printable is that her boss is an old bag. She will be at home if you want to call in. No phone.'

3. 'Charles Maddison of Wintour Garage phoned to tell you that he is sending Earl Parsons back to college because he has been persistently late and un-cooperative.'

4. 'Sandy Matthews phoned to say she is bored and the placement is useless and she doesn't want to carry on. Convinced her to stay until her tutor visited her, which is planned for tomorrow. She agreed.'

5. 'John has phoned in from his visit to Julia Steer at the carpet shop. She said to him privately that she cannot stand all the dirty jokes and foul language and that the boss can't keep his hands to himself. John is bringing her in to college this afternoon.'

6. 'Wendy Powell is waiting for you in your office!!!!'

12. Work Experience within the Curriculum - *Making Integration Work*

The desirability of curriculum integration is widely agreed among teachers. The debate is less on whether this is a good thing than on how to go about achieving it. It is not easy to put together a programme of learning in which topics, tasks, skills and knowledge are clearly and explicitly inter-related, not only on paper but also in the students' actual experience. Many obstacles stand in the way of coherent, integrated curriculum delivery – timetables, resource distribution, entrenched attitudes, time-honoured administrative systems and, above all, subject-based national examinations.

This chapter explores the possibilities of achieving a measure of curriculum integration for and through the work experience component. It looks at ways of linking school/college-based learning with the students' experience in placements. Four methods of working towards this integration are outlined here:

1. Activities and Discussions Centred around Work Experience

The full use of work experience as a learning context by all the staff who teach the students helps to establish connections between work experience and the rest of the curriculum. The interests and expertise of all staff can come into play in preparing students for work experience and subsequently in follow-up activities. For example:

- Writing to placement providers (communication skills teacher);
- Safety at work (science teacher);
- Problem-solving at work (life skills teacher);
- Understanding the workplace (careers teacher).

This style of high-profile teacher involvement in work experience needs to be well co-ordinated so as not to become repetitive and intrusive to the point of being counter-productive. If work experience feels like just another assignment, the young person who saw it as a bridge to an adult world may dismiss much of what could be its value.

well as for future consumers. Helping students to assess the quality of their placement can be a valuable learning experience in itself, developing confidence in their own judgements.

Activities for Students

1. Students write their evaluation of their placement, using criteria agreed earlier, in the preparation stage.

They then look at the notes they made during the preparation activity on page 50 and compare their answers, discussing the developments in their own perceptions.

2. Decide with the class group the stages that were important in preparing for and carrying out work experience placements, and list the different activities or tasks for each stage. For example:

- preparation at college – choosing your placement, preparing for the first visit, rehearsing problems at work;
- work experience placement – induction by the company, the tutor's visit, assessment.

Design a grid in which they rate their own contribution and that of the employer or teacher. For example:

Work experience stages	*Student*	*Employer*	*Teacher*	*Comments*
Preparation – choosing the placement – preparing for the first visit – rehearsing problems at work				

Agree a scale of 1–5 with 1 being the maximum support and participation, and 5 being no support or participation. Encourage the students to comment on why they give the marks they do, either in writing or in a group discussion. Draw out the main points and note them on a flip chart, paper or blackboard.

It can be helpful, before undertaking such a group discussion, to agree ways in which comments can be given honestly and constructively. For example, some of the basic rules of feedback given in assertiveness training can be shared with a group, saying 'I felt . . .' or 'I experienced . . .' or 'I thought . . .' rather than 'You did . . .' or 'You were . . .,' being specific rather than general, 'She never came to see me' rather than 'She was useless'.

Placement Maintenance and Development

Initial negotiations, placement visits, placement evaluation, and receptions for employers are all part of an on-going process of co-operation between employers in the community and the college or school.

Activities for Placement Maintenance and Development

1. Work together with employers, individually or in a group, to develop work-based material and vocationally-based assignments. Some colleges have set up area occupational advisory boards with local employers and may want to ask these boards to undertake this work.

2. Discuss with employers, in groups or individually, areas in which the college or school resources may be of use to them, e.g. training in computers; use of computer and other technical resources; equal opportunities or assessment sessions for their staff.

Education is not limited to the school or college. Increasingly the teacher needs to be able to take on the role of manager of the various resources a community can offer its students – its businesses, amenities, organizations and resources. Work experience is one of the best opportunities to put this partnership into practice. It offers a wider scope for the education of students but also enables teachers to broaden their experiences, and employers the opportunity to contribute to the education of the next generation. Just as work experience can help young people in their transition from school or college into the realities of the wider adult world, so it can offer teachers and employers a forum for co-operation, to their mutual benefit.

14. Alternatives to Work Experience

An alternative activity to work experience may be more appropriate or more practicable in certain circumstances. Work placements are increasingly in demand by schools, colleges and youth training schemes. In some areas demand on local employers is so great that teachers have real difficulty in finding enough placements. On some courses, students may not have reached a point in their development where they can undertake a placement in an unfamiliar setting away from the support of school or college.

If traditional work experience as described in this book is either not available or not appropriate, a range of alternatives to work experience have been developed which can provide useful learning contexts. They cannot offer the same experience as a placement in a company organization in the community, but often they can offer complementary experiences, including opportunities to develop skills in taking responsibility and in working with a group which are not usually available in most traditional placements.

A brief summary of some of the alternatives is given here.

1. Work Simulation

In work simulation, a working environment is created which resembles a real workplace and in which real work tasks are undertaken. A service is provided or a product is manufactured and students take on all the roles required in a small business from managing director to cleaner. Mini-enterprises have included window-cleaning, making sandwiches or cakes to sell in local businesses at lunchtime, providing entertainment for a local playgroup, making cushions, lampshades or soft toys for Christmas.

The simulated workbase can be within the school or college, or in a space locally donated by a church, community centre or local workshop. Some schemes, as the second example shows, extend the concept to include simulation of the total life of a young worker, allowing the students participating in work simulation to share also in the experience of living independently.

Work simulations give students the opportunity to take responsiblity for all aspects of a project and to learn many difficult lessons about working co-operatively. They can be helpful as a way of exploring the possibility of running a small business and being self-employed. Teachers arranging work simulation need to support students not only to achieve their task but to reflect on the process of their working together.

(a) Mini-enterprise

Mini-enterprise situations are designed in which students plan, establish, and run a small company producing goods or delivering services.

The decisions for which students are responsible include the product(s) or service(s), the manufacturing process, the design, the costings, the marketing strategy, and the need for such functions as sales, personnel, secretarial and accounting – all the aspects of a small business. Having decided on the functions involved, they then draw up job descriptions, establishing the conditions of work (including issues of equal opportunities and sanctions), advertising the posts in a simulated bulletin, taking applications, shortlisting, making appointments, and then starting work.

Throughout this process students are supported in their deliberations by resource staff such as teachers, careers officers, personnel officers, youth workers, and members of local businesses and organizations, who are helpful at the interview stage in particular.

(b) Residential and Work Simulation

This model combines living away from home with simulated work experience. Students plan both the work experience and the living away from home elements. Some colleges or schools have residential centres or access to such centres or urban studies bases; others use holiday camps out of season.

Having gone through a preliminary induction at their proposed living quarters, perhaps during a weekend in the month before the project begins, students then work together to plan and set up a small company, through all the stages described above.

The work simulation can be located in a church hall, youth club, empty office or workshop accommodation, or another appropriate place in the vicinity of their living accommodation.

The residential and work simulation is normally in a two to three week block. For the duration, the students live as independent young workers would, taking responsibility for getting up, eating, getting to work on time, arranging for shopping, washing up, and preparing meals.

Teachers and/or youth workers support the group, perhaps taking turns to live-in. Group meetings to plan, discuss and evaluate both their working and domestic arrangements and experiences are an integral part of such a scheme. The students solve together the daily problems they encounter. Such discussions can be videoed for use on return to college/school for further learning and evaluation.

Although many young people may not have the opportunity to live independently, the experience of living away from home and learning to live co-operatively with a group can be a helpful learning experience for the transition they will need to make with their own families in leaving school, even if they do not or cannot leave home.

(c) Computer Simulation

Some work simulations are available through computer packages or interactive video. Such simulations can be a helpful preparation for actual work experience placements. They give students a series of work tasks to complete, e.g. a travel agency simulation programme. Students have to call up information about available flights, hotel accommodation, prices, timetables and insurance.

Although computer simulations can provide realistic work tasks, the student does not get the experience of working with and for other people. Discussion and review sessions amongst the students can help them derive the maximum benefit from this approach.

2. Work Shadowing

In work shadowing students accompany and observe a person at work through all the various tasks he/she undertakes. They become the worker's 'shadow'. Because students can shadow a worker whose job they cannot immediately take on, such as a bank manager or a nurse, they can learn about work in which they might be interested. Work shadowing can offer students of both sexes an opportunity to observe workers in non-traditional roles.

Those who have used this approach find it gives opportunities for learning facts about the workplace, for collecting useful material for project work and evidence for case studies, as well as breaking down some of the stereotypes about jobs and who is suitable for them.

In order for work shadowing to be useful, students need to have a series of structured tasks and observations to undertake. 'Shadowing' needs to be guided and purposeful rather than just 'hanging around'.

3. Worker Tutors

In this alternative to traditional work experience, teachers arrange with local employers for one of more of their staff to meet with a small group of students on a regular basis. The worker tutor discusses with them their own job, the workplace, aspects of working life, finding a job, their job aspirations and anything else the young person might want to know. Together the group embark on activities to gain more information about work and, where appropriate, to help group members in job/training plans and applications, with support from teachers and careers officers who visit the group by arrangement.

The group might meet at the school or at the worker tutor's place of employment or a more neutral setting such as a local community centre. Fact-finding visits to workplaces with the worker tutor can form part of the group's activities. Teachers need to liaise both with the employer and the worker tutor to make sure that the aim of the scheme is clear and that worker tutors know they have support from someone who knows the students well.

4. Using Workshops and Small Business Premises

Local councils in some areas of the country have encouraged the development of craft work and small businesses by taking over large premises and converting them into small units which are let at attractive rents. Under one roof are then assembled a variety of people and enterprises. Schools and colleges already find such workshops fertile ground for placements. It may be possible to develop this idea further for alternatives to work experience. For example:

- some workshops left free to use for work simulations in an adult environment;
- workshops let at discounted rents for businesses willing to provide work experience placements;
- schools/colleges providing support services to the small businesses, e.g. office services or lunchtime catering, as part of a mini-enterprise programme.

5. Enterprise Projects

Provision may be made within the curriculum for students, individually or in groups, to identify and then undertake Enterprise Projects. This would mean having an idea and then seeing it through to completion. The idea might be based in business, improving learning, community work, or planning a residential visit. Such projects enable students to plan, make decisions, accept responsibility, use powers of persuasion, and develop their own motivation to work at a task and see it through to completion.

Further Reading

Eggleston, J. *Work Experience in Secondary Schools*. Routledge, 1982

Holmes, S., Jamieson, I. and Perry, J. *Work Experience in the School Curriculum*. SCIP, 1983

Jamieson, I., Miller, A. and Watts, A. G. *Mirrors of Work*. Falmer, 1988

Watts, A. G. *Work Experience and Schools*. Heinemann, 1983

Jamieson, I. *We Make Kettles – Studying Industry in Primary School.* Longman, 1984

Jamieson, I. *Industry in Education*. Longman, 1985

Sims, David. *The TVE1 Experience: Views from Teacher and Students*: 'Work Experience in TVE1, Students Views and Reactions – A Preliminary Study' in NFER National Evaluation Team. July 1987.

Experience, Reflection, Learning. Further Education Unit (FEU), 1978

National Vocational Qualifications – Criteria and Procedures. National Council for Vocational Qualifications, March 1989